M.A.R.I.A.201001000

sean::adrian::brijbasi

Published simultaneously in the United States
and Great Britain in 2022
by Pretend Genius
Copyright © Sean::Adrian::Brijbasi

This book is copyright under the Berne
Convention
No reproduction without permission
All rights reserved

ISBN: 979-8-9859089-2-3

other books by Sean::Adrian::Brijbasi

One Note Symphonies
for Emma

Still Life in Motion
*for those who play
Marius and Andréus*

The Unknowed Things
for Julius

The Dictionary of Coincidences, Volume i
for Emma

S{E}AN?
for EM{M}A+

E{M}MA+ the ghost orchids
for Emma

darling two hearts
for E{M}MA+ the ghost orchids

Stories for Nadira
*for Adrian, Andréus, Elijah, Helena, Julius,
Marius, Nadira*

Play Championship World-Class
Tennis with Bjorn McEnroe
*for Adrian, Andréus, Elijah, Helena, Julius,
Marius, Nadira*

The World That Destroyed the World
*for Adrian, Andréus, Elijah, Helena, Julius,
Marius, Nadira*

The Book of Lashonda
*for Adrian, Andréus, Elijah, Helena, Julius,
Marius, Nadira*

ENTROPALACE
for my brother Troy

NO ONE CAN SEE THE WORLD I LIVE
IN
for the only one

for

my sister

Simone

Au milieu de l'hiver, j'apprenais enfin qu'il y avait en moi un été invincible.

--AC

CONTENTS

1

M.A.R.I.A.201001000

M.A.R.I.A.201001010

100. M

1. I forget who I am but the leaves remind me.
2. I don't usually stop to look at them.
3. But they're always around me.
4. The ones on the ground can be crushed.
5. Sometimes I see pieces of them beneath recently fallen leaves which can also be crushed.
6. To look like part of the concrete.
7. I look up to the leaves still on the trees.
8. In autumn when they're different colors and blowing in the wind.
9. Old leaves (the "dying") though they seem younger than spring leaves (the "living")—like children who don't sit still.
10. Pointing in the same direction, like a million arrows.

99. A

11. But they fall like horses.
12. Held back by old hands 'til they can't be held back no more.
13. And tumble legs first.
14. Kicking and bucking in the sundry breezes.
15. Pivoting on irregular and changing axes.
16. When they land it's not the fields I imagine for them.
17. Just the ground and they're only leaves.
18. In the city they get the shoe sole or the rubber tire.
19. In the country, the cow, the horse, and the goat hoof.
20. And in the old days (in the city and the country) the iron plow share and the wooden wagon wheel.

98. R

21. But the summer leaves remind me of Maria.
22. Moving her hair away from her face.
23. At dusk with her delicate hand.
24. In the dim light of another room.
25. I see her from far away.
26. A secret like a drop of rain hiding a deeper ocean.
27. That people pass by on the sidewalk.
28. No one would ever know and I don't tell.
29. I can't tell—anyone.
30. Not even her.

97. I

31. Sometimes she plays a nocturne on a badly tuned piano.
32. Each measure, a passage to a thousand miles of neural pathways.

33. Or a million, connecting the moment in which it is heard (in which I hear it) to everything good and bad.
34. Or what I consider good and bad to be.
35. And then the rain—spattering the window and the rough sea it came from, hundreds of miles away.
36. When she finishes, she closes the fallboard over the keys, and rests her hands on the polished mahogany as if it were a coffin.
37. The moment buried inside of it.
38. Sometimes she doesn't play but sits quietly and waits for me to ask and when I do—as I do—she starts before I finish speaking.
39. The nocturne, like the sun shines in my dreams—always dark, always sad.
40. Or what I consider darkness and sadness to be.

96. A

41. I could ask her to play a song that shines like the sun in real life but she'll raise her hand to me.
42. A conductor quieting the brass section so the interplay of winds outside can be heard.
43. I think she'd rather be alone with something beautiful (or what she considers beautiful) than be happy with me.
44. But I could be beautiful too.
45. Beautiful for me and beautiful for other people.
46. Like Maria, who other people love and who is beautiful for them.
47. We could sit together without speaking.
48. Aware of each other, like we are aware of a soft breeze when our eyes are closed.

49. In the same room.
50. And then in different rooms.

95. M

51. But it was in this room she heard the news.
52. Her sister had gone away.
53. The two words: she's gone.
54. Which made her ask out loud: *where did she go?*
55. And which she took to mean her sister had awakened before everyone, packed her bag, and got on a train to somewhere.
56. The two words that made her think she needed to think of different places her sister might go.
57. Or go to the train station before the train arrived and meet her on the platform.

58. Tell her to come back because everything would be okay.
59. Maybe go with her if she didn't stay.
60. And then call to tell everyone she had packed a bag also and would be returning after a few days.

94. A

61. But then she understood the meaning of the two words, so that all she could think about was the last time she saw her sister.
62. When her sister waved good-bye from the path across the field.
63. After a good day of good things built on top of good things.
64. I remember Maria waving—remember the next day and every day after.
65. How she waved with her whole arm.
66. As if to say: *we have met and we shall meet again.*

67. *We think of each other as if we belong together but can't always be.*
68. I was there but didn't wave, didn't grasp the intricacies of the gesture.
69. Maria might have seen me out of the corner of her eye as I watched them.
70. Like a moon in her orbit as the day's light dimmed and the sun set on the path across the field.

93. R

71. And then a few weeks after the two words.
72. I'm sitting in the room next to the room.
73. Still in orbit around Maria.
74. She sits at the piano and plays her nocturne.
75. And then she closes the fallboard, rests her hands there, and lowers her head.

76. It's the first time I see her crying—her tears stream down her face and wet the polished mahogany.
77. I can't think of anything to do but leave.
78. But she hears me and wipes the piano with her sleeve.
79. I don't see her cry again but sometimes hear her playing from my apartment below, early in the morning, when it's still dark.
80. And then the silence, palpable, like a small pocket of time in which I think she keeps the essence of her grief.

92. I

81. I don't think I can help Maria.
82. I can only talk about my memories of her sister—about this time or that time.

83. About how we talked one winter morning about the rain water freezing and breaking the asphalt on the road.
84. How the small droplets infiltrate the thinnest fissures and drip by drip settle into a pool beneath.
85. Then freeze, expand, thaw, contract, and leave a hole there that weakens the entire structure so that if, by spring, the weakness went untreated, the entire structure would collapse.
86. I was waiting at the bus stop outside the apartment when she saw me.
87. We talked for a few minutes and then the bus arrived.
88. She continued walking, bundled up in a scarf and winter jacket I've seen Maria wearing since.
89. On cold days and on days when it wasn't cold.

90. Though, it could be argued, the seasons were in transition.

91. A

91. I was turned away from the road and couldn't tell if she saw me watching Maria's apartment window.
92. Watching for a light to go on because I worried irrationally.
93. Worried that Maria had stopped breathing during the night.
94. Because I hadn't heard the piano in the morning.
95. Or somehow her heart had stopped beating for no reason.
96. It seemed like such an easy thing for something so small in something so fragile to do.
97. Or she lay on her bed in the dark.
98. Unsure of the day.

99. Turning on her side to look at the same window I looked at.

100. Thinking of the simplest things to do until it was dark again when she could go back to sleep.

90. M

101. And the dream she said she had dreamed many times.

102. The dream she had on that first day after the two words.

103. Described to me once though I felt she only gave a synopsis as if the telling was a trial to see how much she could tell.

104. Leaving out those details in dreams we might put into words but choose not to.

105. Because they reveal too much—even to those we love—about things we don't understand.

106. The dream about turning on the light in the room to find her sister.

107. And colliding against the walls, the bed frame, the bedside table, the books, and the lamp to get near her.

108. The hard journey.

109. And then the feeling she always felt—of trying—even as she did nothing, as she said nothing, on that day and every day.

110. An infinite trying, beyond all hope and logic, against a great and unyielding power.

89. A

111. Then the morning after the two words.

112. Though I didn't know yet—hadn't gotten the news.

113. When I heard Maria's voice, thinking it was the same voice I heard the day before.

114. On the day we were supposed to take the bus together.

115. And I watched for the light in the window because she hadn't come out yet.

116. Then I saw the light in the window, saw the curtains drawn, saw Maria lift open the window.

117. I walked a few steps across the road to her.

118. I remember how many.

119. I still count them in my head when I walk or when I see others walk.

120. But she said don't wait for me, I can't come.

88. R

121. We were teenagers the first time I saw her.
122. I remember it like an important memory.
123. Waiting, with many others, for the train that would take us to the summer camp.
124. Our last year because we were getting too old.
125. Already too old.
126. She had one foot on the table in front of her seat and I saw the sole of her shoe.
127. Saw the scratches and scuffmarks there that made me look up to her face.
128. As sunlight shone into the big windows in the great hall of the train station.

129. I saw her smiling in a way that made me think she had a secret.

130. Unnoticeable unless drawn to it by something else.

87. I

131. I looked around to see if others noticed.

132. But kept her in my periphery.

133. Because I had a secret too.

134. I didn't see her again for a long time.

135. When I did, I said I thought she looked familiar.

136. She said she didn't know me.

137. And I was happy because it was better to know me when she did and not earlier.

138. When I knew less of everything.

139. When I was unremarkable.

140. And when neither of us would have remembered how it all ended.

86. A

141. I watched from the window on the night they came to take her sister's things.
142. Saw others watching from their windows.
143. Saw her father and brother take the bedframe and mattress.
144. In the night because it was dark.
145. I stood behind the curtain.
146. Heard them speaking.
147. More softly than quietly.
148. Navigating the bedframe through the open door.
149. And tried not to imagine this was the bed they found her on.
150. Or how her body lay across it.

85. M

151. Maria saw me.
152. Or she saw the curtain move.

153. And I withdrew to the sofa.
154. Then a knock on my door—a soft knock that I would come to know as hers.
155. She walked through the room and sat at the small kitchen table.
156. I looked out the window again and thought I heard her ask if she could stay.
157. I wasn't sure—couldn't be sure—in that strange quiet of the night.
158. When language takes the shape of sleep and the dreams we half-remember.
159. When all the people outside have gone.
160. And all the watchers have turned off their lights.

84. A

161. Maria can't be happy with me because she's not herself when she's happy.
162. But she can be herself with me because I say nothing and I do nothing.
163. I breathe quietly near her.
164. Sometimes move my arms and legs.
165. In return I get something beautiful.
166. A painting on afternoons when she falls asleep on the sofa.
167. A sculpture when she sits by the window to watch the rain.
168. A dance when she turns and descends the stairs to leave.
169. And a woman when she looks at me as if she wants to speak.
170. But says nothing.

83. R

171. I can't get any closer.

172. One day she'll meet someone.

173. A good man who loves her.

174. They'll talk about the weather and the birds in the yard.

175. Ask each other about tea.

176. And in thirty years, I'll wonder if she thinks about the time we spent together.

177. Or maybe she'll be ashamed (though she shouldn't be).

178. So that if we should meet again, she'll say it was so long ago that she hardly remembers.

179. *Did I play the piano every morning?*

180. *How did you put up with me?*

82. I

181. And I'll think it wasn't so long ago.

182. Then sum the years up in my head and accept that it was.

183. But I'll have a yard too.

184. And I'll know about birds.

185. I'll see them ascending from between the green leaves of the maple tree outside her window.
186. And call them out by genus and species.
187. *Loxia cardinalis* and *passus domesticus*.
188. She'll tell her husband how clever I've always been.
189. But I'll tell her I'd been planning for this moment since the day she left.
190. Or I'll think the words but say instead: *I only know those two—they're very common.*

81. A

191. Or maybe in ten years, we'll think our time together couldn't have lasted.
192. And remember it like we remember something we used to buy at the grocery store—that one summer.

193. But I think I'll remember it differently.

194. Alone in my happy house.

195. The look on my face changing when I'm reminded.

196. By the way the winter air hits my skin on certain mornings.

197. Or by the sound of a bus that stops to let on more passengers before starting off again.

198. And I'll grow a certain way.

199. I'll become elegant.

200. She would have done this.

80. M

201. Sometimes I hate the sadness of life.

202. The way we try to find meaning in everything bad that happens.

203. Move in our own heads when we're moving in the world.

204. And look for signs that everything will be alright.
205. In the bird that lands on the railing and lingers too long.
206. Or the balloon that floats above the tree line across the way.
207. Wouldn't it be better to not remember Maria?
208. To walk into a room wearing your favorite dress.
209. One or both shoulders bare.
210. And your eyes on everyone.

79. A

211. But her eyes were on no one as she lay around my apartment.
212. Sometimes curled up on her side beneath a blanket.
213. Pretending to be asleep.
214. Turned away from the door I leave ajar.

215. Just enough to see that she's okay.

216. She'd be talking to her sister now.

217. I feel it in the silence of the day.

218. Like a hand that pulls my shirt from behind.

219. To stop me from going to her.

220. She'll come out when she's ready.

78. R

221. I'll hear her footsteps.

222. Hear the apartment door closing as she leaves.

223. On some days, she'll stay.

224. I won't know why.

225. But I prepare as if she will always stay.

226. So we can be quietly around each other.

227. And hope the noise from the road or the people who live next door isn't too loud.

228. Though it's better when there is a little noise.

229. Now and then.

230. To make us look at each other for a moment and wonder.

77. I

231. I don't know what she wonders.

232. I wonder different things.

233. Maybe the same as her.

234. I wonder what happened to her sister.

235. I wonder how long she's going to stay.

236. I wonder if she's coming back tomorrow.

237. Sometimes I wonder about the noises we hear.

238. The murmurs in the hallway.

239. The clattering in the apartment next door.

240. I wonder if they will lead to something.

76. A

241. Something we can talk about.

242. Or take part in.

243. Something good that connects us and makes us happy when we remember.

244. Something to balance out the melancholy always around us.

245. Because she and I are a like a sad family.

246. Who only talk about one thing when we talk about everything.

247. A million different words spoken in a million different ways but all the same.

248. Or are they orphan moments like most moments?

249. Connected only as a matter of sequence and not in any meaningful way.

250. Because this is how and where they occurred in the chain of a human life.

75. M

251. I remember the day Maria helped me take off my shoe.
252. I sat on the floor of the dimly lit entrance by the apartment door.
253. The sneaker stuck on my right foot because I hadn't loosened the strings.
254. I had just come in from the rain and didn't know she was there.
255. She would have seen the shoe was still wet.
256. She went to the kitchen and wiped her hands with a towel.
257. Brought the same towel to me and dried my face.
258. And I thought all my sweetest dreams.

259. My sweetest dreams for a thousand years of sleep.

260. Couldn't compare to that one moment I was awake.

74. A

261. I don't know what to do.

262. I think the trees know.

263. They look at me as if they do.

264. As if they know I don't understand what they're trying to tell me.

265. Yet still try.

266. Some try harder.

267. The young ones.

268. Their leaves frantic in the softest breeze.

269. Because the old ones already know.

270. That I will never learn their language.

73. R

271. The clouds know too.

272. And laugh at me.

273. From above like so many.

274. As they drift along and disappear my shadow from the earth.

275. The only thing left that's whole.

276. That has the shape of a human.

277. I know I can't hide everything from them.

278. But I can hide some things.

279. Turn my body sideways to the trunk of an old tree (or a young one).

280. And hide my shadow in its own.

72. I

281. But the summer leaves remind me of you Maria.

282. I watch them from my window.

283. Watch you standing by the fence beneath the trees.

284. Your hand resting on a piece of wood.

285. Made of them.

286. And I feel happy.

287. To think you might be walking around here in fifty years.

288. Somewhere in your pajamas and bare feet.

289. While our bodies break down.

290. And our minds fall apart.

71. A

291. Though I think we'd still have enough left to take us all the way.

292. Color inside the disappearing outlines of what we remember.

293. Sometimes exacting in our shades of blues and greens.

294. Of the sky between the high oaks and evergreens.

295. And the high oaks and evergreens themselves.

296. Or the feeble yellows of the lights that come through our windows as we sleep.

297. And more, sometimes bleeding outside the faint and blurring outlines.
298. To pull us towards other forms we can no longer see.
299. No matter how bright.
300. Like a fuse that burns but doesn't…

70. M

301. We'd still have enough left to take us all the way.
302. Wouldn't we Maria?
303. Look at each other and remember.
304. Remember for each other.
305. So that together we remember everything.
306. Or would everything leave us to remain here?
307. As we travel towards oblivion.
308. Without the strength to carry a single atom between us.
309. For now, we have all of this.

310. More than we can lift.

69. A

311. We're going anyway.

312. And all the way.

313. We can be certain of that if nothing else.

314. *We all end up the same.*

315. She said the words to me as if I didn't know.

316. Or maybe she had never thought about it before.

317. Because she didn't have to.

318. And maybe it was better that way.

319. To not be tempted by the thought of turning the car into the ravine.

320. Or taking one more step into the fast lane.

68. R

321. How can people be happy she would ask me.

322. As we strolled past the clothes shops and restaurants.

323. As if she wasn't one of them.

324. And I would answer I don't know Maria.

325. As if I wasn't either.

326. And out of the blue she might buy a dress at one of the clothes shops.

327. Or stop for a drink at one of the restaurants.

328. Watch the small trucks and vans unload their goods onto the street.

329. Around the people who buy such things.

330. And put her cup down without looking at me.

67. I

331. She'd tell me she heard her sister cry every night.

332. Every night she wiped the window glass with her sleeve.

333. Or cleaned it with one of the socks she picked up from the floor.

334. Then to bed when she'd pretend to be asleep.

335. And hear her sister.

336. Think of reaching over to her but instead stir.

337. So that she might stop.

338. Or turn around to tell her what was wrong.

339. Maybe she'd seen a sad movie—that was all.

340. Because Maria didn't know what to do.

66. A

341. Sometimes her sister would spy the clock.

342. Get up and look through the window to see clouds drifting across the sky.

343. To another place.

344. And feel the cold air coming through the glass on her warm skin.

345. Take a path to the furthest distance from their room.

346. And open the fridge door.

347. Where the light from inside shined on her legs and feet.

348. In the otherwise dark house.

349. All that could be seen of her from the stairs.

350. If anyone followed.

65. M

351. She was like a different species at night.

352. Hiding in spaces that existed only at night.

353. That were bare and open during the day.
354. Seen by everyone.
355. She sat there.
356. And there.
357. Where the glow from a streetlamp shining through the window.
358. Reached the other side of the room.
359. To light up her pupils.
360. So that she would recede further into the dark.

64. A

361. Maria was like her now.
362. It was her nature and evolution.
363. To grow in a deep and interesting way.
364. Her legs crossed in living rooms and waiting rooms.
365. Her hands together on her lap—fingers clasped.

366. Sitting off to the side like her sister.

367. Around people but not of them.

368. Then one day she got up and left—disappeared.

369. Just like that without a word.

370. And all the disbelief from people who couldn't imagine leaving everything behind.

63. R

371. It's not like she's leaving the Earth I'd say.

372. She's off on an adventure.

373. Something that would make your heart race if you were so brave.

374. She'll come back one day and tell us all about it.

375. Though, in time, I understood that adventure was too simple a word.

376. Too perfect.

377. For a too-perfect story to be told after a long absence.

378. Or an observation that ends for the observer but continues for the observed.

379. After we're compelled by a puncture in the bicycle tire or an official-looking envelope pushed through the mail slot.

380. To go on about our day.

62. I

381. And we would.

382. Go on about our day.

383. She'd take my hand and lead me down a new street.

384. Then let it go once we were safely in.

385. Where the sidewalks looked and felt (under our feet) of new material.

386. Innovations in concrete and metal science.

387. Used in different parts of the city.

388. Something about chemical bonding and elastic properties.
389. I had glanced the words in the newspaper.
390. We'd have to walk on the sidewalk across the road while they worked over here.

61. A

391. That's what I thought on that first day.
392. Because I was unsure of what would happen next.
393. But we just walked.
394. And occasionally tell each other to look at something.
395. The forgotten umbrella leaning against the inside corner of the bus stop shelter.
396. The black cat sitting in the upper-floor apartment window.

397. And each time down a new street she'd take my hand.

398. Then let it go once we were safely in.

399. I tried to memorize the street names.

400. So that next time I'd know the ones we had walked down again that she had forgotten.

60. M

401. But they weren't as easy to memorize as the genus and species of two birds.

402. I'd remember them for a while.

403. Maybe until that night.

404. But the next day I'd forget.

405. And all my plans to wander the city by myself.

406. So I could lead her down interesting paths.

407. Never materialized.

408. I would have been a real cosmopolitan then.

409. People would stop and ask me where they could find this or that.

410. And right in front of her—pointing off in the distance—I would tell them.

59. A

411. Sometimes I felt like we'd been down a street before.

412. Something about the crimson color of a sign.

413. Or the way it hung from the worn brick above the doorway of a shop.

414. Opened the year before I was born.

415. The feeling of uncertainty I had grown up with.

416. That had grown up with me.

417. Of always grasping for a thing but not grasping it.

418. Because certain things unsettled me.

419. Because the way certain things felt in my hands.

420. Made me feel like dropping them.

58. R

421. We walked every day until the weather changed.

422. Until it became too warm to wear her sister's coat.

423. The one she wore the day we rode the bus.

424. I'd look out the window and see another spring.

425. Imagine ourselves as free creatures moving in that warm air.

426. Petals from flowering trees falling around our heads.

427. And I'd think about going out there without her.

428. Then glimpse the white doily on the table by the window.

429. Marked with a circle from the drinking glass.

430. I had thoughtlessly placed on it a few days before.

57. I

431. She'd find a book there after I left.
432. Hiding what I'd done.
433. Because I didn't know how to fix it—my blunder.
434. Against the beautifully ordered world she created.
435. Maybe she'd pick the book up and see the mark.
436. Place it back on her bookshelf.
437. So that when I returned, I'd know all had been revealed.
438. Or maybe she'd put it back exactly as I left it.
439. So that when I picked it up again.
440. I'd see the mark was gone.

56. A

441. It wouldn't be any book.

442. I'd select something meaningful.

443. With a cover that complemented (in its own way) the nearby surroundings.

444. In this case—the window, the sky, the doily—something of the stratosphere.

445. Sometimes she appeared after a few days.

446. Like a being that was only just forming.

447. Who had purged her brain without sorting the good from the bad.

448. So that when I remarked with a slack smile.

449. About the amusing incident from the last time we were together.

450. It seemed as if she didn't hear me.

55. M

451. As if she were working something out in her head.

452. I'd get serious to match her.

453. And she'd take the book and study the back cover.
454. *Have I read this one?*
455. *Have you read it?*
456. And if I said yes or sometimes nodded.
457. She'd place the book on top of her piano with the others she hadn't read.
458. Not just anywhere but on a certain space.
459. Because the weight of its hundred pages.
460. Changed the piano's timbre and tone.

54. A

461. So that when she played.
462. She searched the air for a new sound.
463. While I searched her face for a look of recognition.
464. Every day without her killed almost all of me.

465. How meaningless they were.

466. Maybe it was the same for her.

467. And it didn't matter what she did or didn't do.

468. Or said or didn't say.

469. I only knew that when we were together.

470. She wouldn't kill what was left.

53. R

471. And I would remain.

472. What I am as someone.

473. Becoming who they really are.

474. In the face of all of this.

475. In the eyes and mouth and the faintest impressions.

476. Of lines not yet formed.

477. After so many false starts and stops.

478. And missteps to try again.

479. And again.

480. Until the end.

52. I

481. But I could only imagine what Maria felt.

482. The heat alone burned.

483. My skin and flesh down to the bone.

484. And sometimes the bone to the marrow.

485. While the fire it came from.

486. Burned all of her.

487. And left her as nothing but ashes.

488. To live in this blustery world.

489. That scattered her.

490. So that she was never whole.

51. A

491. I felt as if I gathered her up from everywhere.

492. It's the reason I was there.

493. Even in her mostly dark room.

494. Although sometimes there was enough light coming from other rooms.

495. To see her eyes over the cup brim.

496. As I watched her drink tea.

497. Wild like the eyes of animal that stopped for a moment to rest.

498. Hunted and haunted.

499. By something only known to her.

500. As despair.

50. M

501. She thought she was happy.

502. Before her sister went away.

503. It was better to be happy.

504. So many people had told her.

505. And she'd still suffer her fair share.

506. As much as any other happy person.

507. From the common sufferings.

508. From the sympathizing with others who weren't happy.

509. Put herself into it and imagine it hard.

510. So she could understand people who weren't happy.

49. A

511. Like her.

512. Because there was a time not so long ago.

513. When it didn't make sense (the thought didn't exist).

514. As she watched children play.

515. On the playgrounds beneath trees.

516. On the uncut and endless fields.

517. That one strange day.

518. And every day after.

519. They would have to be encouraged.

520. To live.

48. R

521. But I thought despite everything.

522. She wouldn't want to be someone else.

523. Someone who didn't recognize beauty.

524. In little things.

525. Hear all the sounds.

526. A song had to offer.

527. Or sense the pulse of the universe.

528. And see how people like her sister.

529. Got lost in the imagined silence.

530. Between beats.

47. I

531. Nothing distracted her from the absence.

532. And some things, once added.

533. Multiplied it.

534. Like today and the next day.

535. No sounds or colors or textures.

536. Filled it.

537. There was never enough of anything.

538. Except the almost-silence.

539. Of her preferred room upstairs.

540. In the furthest corner from the front door.

46. A

541. As if it were difficult to find.

542. As if the people who passed by from outside.

543. Couldn't see the window and think someone lives there.

544. And the droning from the fan above.

545. Attuned with a coded message for her.

546. And for those like her.

547. Translated by her body.

548. As an inconceivable pain.

549. Though the breeze from it felt good.

550. And helped her fall asleep.

45. M

551. She could fill the absence there.

552. With things not yet created.

553. Born new into the world.

554. I'd listen outside the door but never open it.

555. Walk away and practice my knock.

556. On the door of a different room.

557. Imagine she would answer.

558. So I would open the door and stand in the doorway for a moment.

559. Then walk through the darkness to the window.

560. To part the curtains and let the sunlight in.

44. A

561. I'd sit there on the window ledge.

562. And lean my back against the glass.

563. Try to think about existence.

564. But think about nothing.

565. And wonder if or what other people think.

566. Then search the door, the door frame, or the door knob.

567. Or the light shining on the wood floor.

568. For something beautiful.

569. And through the window feel the warmth on my neck.

570. From a radiance more associated with life.

43. R

571. Than with death

572. And feel shame.

573. For thinking how beautiful life is, after all.

574. Even though I didn't want to believe it.

575. But felt compelled for some reason to think it.

576. Precisely then.

577. Maybe it was the window behind me.

578. And the two stories.

579. Far enough down to break my neck.

580. If I didn't brace myself for the fall.

42. I

581. Or maybe it was the woman in the nearby room.
582. Whose beauty left me dumb.
583. Who said she loved her sister.
584. In a way that made me think she didn't love anything.
585. Or anyone else.
586. But people didn't need.
587. To love a thing to keep it around.
588. I once had a dog I only liked.
589. And that, in the end, I put down.
590. Out of kindness.

41. A

591. I buried it in the backyard.
592. And planted a rose bush on top of it.
593. Maria said her sister's favorite flower was the lotus.
594. And hers was the water lily.
595. The giant ones in South America.

596. They had seen them in the geography book.
597. They would read together on the floor of their bedroom.
598. In the dark mornings before their parents called out to wake them.
599. Or so she said one night when she stayed at my apartment.
600. And later fell asleep on the sofa.

40. M

601. When I could imagine.
602. The sofa was a giant water lily.
603. Floating her body down a river.
604. Into which she could dip her hand.
605. To scoop out a drink.
606. That made her forget.
607. I had to leave early the next morning.
608. And on the bus, I imagined her wandering my apartment.

609. And turning on the faucet in the kitchen.

610. To fill a cup with water.

39. A

611. That might have come from a river.

612. And drinking.

613. But not forgetting.

614. And leaving the cup in the sink.

615. Under the dripping faucet.

616. Filled halfway by the time I returned.

617. And that I washed for her.

618. And placed upside down.

619. On the stainless steel.

620. To drink from again.

38. R

621. She said her parents called out to them.

622. In the same order every time.

623. Maria first because she was older.

624. And she wondered if one morning.

625. Or night.

626. They might not change the order.

627. So that she and her sister might answer.

628. On the first call.

629. Or be too surprised.

630. To answer at all.

37. I

631. Though they never did.

632. And always called Maria first and then her sister.

633. And always when they were in the middle.

634. Of reading something about the pyramids in Guatemala.

635. Or the rune stones in Scandinavia.

636. Though it was a small photograph.

637. Of a rose bush that stretched down.

638. A country road in Ecuador.

639. According to the italicized caption.

640. That Maria's sister liked the most.

36. A

641. They would turn back to that page.

642. Every other morning.

643. And know the sun had risen.

644. When a sliver of light.

645. Shined bright on the left margin by Maria's hand.

646. When she would move the book a little to the left.

647. So that the light shined on whatever picture they were looking at.

648. She had lost track of the book.

649. Like people lose track of books.

650. But how and when, she couldn't remember.

35. M

651. The thought would sometimes flash in her mind to find it again.

652. Look in the same places she had already looked.
653. A familiar and odd feeling of small spaces and humidity.
654. For a house, her parents no longer lived in.
655. Maybe she had overlooked.
656. And missed the letter her sister hid inside.
657. Found eleven years later in a yard-sale bin by someone who wanted to see.
658. What the world looked like back then.
659. When life was better.
660. And written in a script only Maria could understand.

34. A.

661. Though easily decipherable by experts in that sort of thing.

662. Using frequency analysis and the coincidence index.
663. To reveal the precision of her suffering.
664. And the years she spent trying.
665. To diffuse it in the morning with music or painting.
666. Or forget it at night with drink and meaningless conversation.
667. Then sleep.
668. And how in the end, overflowing and understanding all.
669. She could do nothing.
670. But something as fantastic and inconceivable as life itself.

33. R

671. Every day a new day.
672. But nothing new to replace the old.
673. And every day, the old still unresolved.

674. Her letter finally read but not read by Maria.

675. Kept by the woman who purchased the book for her daughter.

676. As a curiosity.

677. Like the Sumerian script that, finally translated, described how many goats.

678. One family owed to another.

679. For the accidental killing of a child.

680. But for which no confirmation of payment was ever found.

32. I

681. There was no way to repay Maria.

682. She could only borrow.

683. To make up for the deficit.

684. A little light that reached her.

685. From passing stars.

686. To brighten the dark spaces she lived in.

687. And me as a piece moved.

688. At her desire.

689. To dim any surplus that bared too much.

690. Or shined too brightly in her eyes.

31. A

691. To blind her from things as they are.

692. In time, I moved myself.

693. In ways that kept her from the glare.

694. Leaned forward on the bus.

695. Or held up a book by the café window.

696. That cast a shadow on her face.

697. To keep her hidden.

698. From the do-gooders and aspiring do-gooders.

699. Who opened doors.

700. And turned on lights.

30. M

701. And who wanted her to get on with it.

702. For everyone to see.

703. Because there was no better way of getting on with it.

704. For her birthday I gave her a vase.

705. That she put on her bookshelf but didn't use.

706. For a long time.

707. And then one day.

708. I saw she had moved it to a different place.

709. And filled with a few plastic flowers.

710. That she must have gone to the store to buy.

29. A

711. And then another day—I don't remember when.

712. I brought a rose from a nearby flower shop.

713. The florist said it had come all the way from Ecuador.

714. But the vase was missing.

715. Or not in its familiar place.

716. I searched the room while she spoke.

717. The bookshelf, the kitchen table, the windowsill.

718. Then silence before she spoke again to say.

719. The vase had broken while she exchanged.

720. The plastic flowers.

28. R

721. For real ones she had picked.

722. From a patch of grass across the road.

723. So what difference did it make?

724. Plastic or real.

725. There was nothing left to fill.

726. The fractured pieces were in the sink.

727. If I wanted to study them.

728. Or put them back together.

729. She had tried but failed.

730. And then she took the rose from my hand.

27. I

731. As if she had just then noticed it.
732. Like something that fell beneath her seat.
733. In a dark and sold-out theatre hall.
734. And instead of returning it to her pocket.
735. Held onto it so it wouldn't fall again.
736. Loose at first then very tight.
737. Until the play ended.
738. Until she made her way through the crowd.
739. And into the empty space of the world.
740. To wait for the #23 bus that would take her home.

26. A

741. She'd walk past me to her room and close the door.//
742. I would hear her though she tried.
743. And I thought it would cause no harm to anyone.
744. If she cried at this time of night.
745. And her tears rained on the world.
746. A light rain that prevented nothing from proceeding as planned.
747. In the same way life goes on from one moment to another.
748. Even when a moment ends for one but not for another.
749. When dust travels in light as always.
750. But new dust in new light.

25. M

751. When a bird hits the window to start.
752. The first beat of a new but weaker heart.

753. And the glass of water left on the table.

754. Like an unmarked headstone.

755. Poured by someone who didn't yet understand the need to live.

756. With an unquenchable thirst.

757. She'd leave it there for her last word.

758. The proper noun no one said to her anymore.

759. When before they said it without thinking.

760. And that she could hear without thinking.

24. A

761. And which she still said to herself.

762. A hundred times a day.

763. So she could hear it in the world.

764. But someone would pour the water out.

765. And wash the glass to save her the trouble.

766. Dry it with the white towel she'd hung for drying.

767. Then open the cupboard for the plates.

768. Close it quietly and search for the right place.

769. Because no one wanted to ask her.

770. Where the glasses go.

23. R

771. She'd always be with her now that she wasn't there.

772. Talk to her every day.

773. Instead of several times a week.

774. Think of her every time she closed her eyes.

775. Instead of finding peace.

776. And try to dream of her though she never did.

777. Her shadow always there.

778. When before it arrived only with the sun.

779. The way she moved—the shadow of every movement.

780. The sound of her voice—the shadow of every voice.

22. I

781. And her hand—the shadow that reached for her hand.

782. That fooled Maria into getting far enough up.

783. From where she had fallen.

784. To raise herself the rest of the way.

785. To breathe and go on until she fell again.

786. And on the way down, thinking.

787. That while others lived for those around them.

788. She lived for those beneath.

789. I could see her falling.

790. Between the go-getters and window-shoppers.

21. A

791. Between the people who strolled through art museums.

792. And sat on park benches and drank cool drinks on hot days.

793. Children saw her too.

794. From the carousel as it took them 'round.

795. Or as their parents held their hands in the ice cream line.

796. As she came to rest like a loose piece of paper.

797. On the fringes of the grass then carried to another place.

798. By the breeze or a gust of air from someone running or a passing car.

799. A page torn from a book of sad poems and her poem.

800. The saddest of all.

20. M

801. But a child might let go of his mother's hand.

802. And follow the page from the fringes of the grass.

803. As it landed for a moment here then there.

804. Read in parts by passersby who spied a word or sentence.

805. But not read in whole.

806. And for a time, though sad, a happy thing.

807. Become part of a child's game.

808. Fleeing, hiding, fleeing again.

809. Taken by a breeze and then by a wind.

810. Above the river's water but never in it.

19. A

811. As if it were carried aloft by the invisible hand.
812. Of an invisible woman who walked along the riverbed.
813. And who placed the page at the feet.
814. Of another woman standing on the bridge above.
815. As the mother took her child by his hand.
816. And walked him back to the playground, though too late.
817. To keep the image of the woman reading whatever was written on that page.
818. The breeze blowing her hair around her face.

819. And the hem of her dress above her knees.

820. From making him feel like he'd never felt before.

18. R

821. She would be an old woman now.

822. But she was still young when I forgot her.

823. And the color of the dress she wore.

824. Or if it was her hair or the loose ribbons of a hat.

825. That blew around her face.

826. Or a flag flown somewhere behind her to celebrate the day.

827. I only sense the feeling of her standing alone.

828. On the bridge above the river.

829. And only when a breeze blows through the room.

830. As I'm falling asleep but know I should stay awake.

17. I

831. It's there that I talk to the dead.

832. Though never a conversation.

833. Thoughts fight along the way.

834. Words and letters tangle until no longer clear.

835. Then silence.

836. In a place that makes me feel.

837. I'm at the limit of life.

838. Where I meet all of life, even death.

839. With a great longing.

840. To call out someone's name.

16. A

841. To ask the questions.

842. Is that you and why did you go?

843. And to hear the answers I want to hear.

844. *Yes* and *I wouldn't go again.*

845. *Not if I knew.*

846. But then someone calls out my name.

847. Someone I love.

848. And I return to the middle from where the threshold.

849. Feels far away.

850. With grocery stores and cars and people eating at restaurants in between.

15. M

851. And I work out that the words were mine.

852. Not someone else's.

853. Spoken in my head by a voice I won't forget.

854. And then questions from downstairs.

855. Are you ready and are you going?

856. *Yes and no* and *yes and no*.

857. The same questions I might ask Maria after putting on my shoes.

858. And opening the front door.

859. To go out there in the middle of it all.

860. To go and go and go.

14. A

861. Like we always go.

862. Though not always in the right order.

863. Drawn away from the sorrow for a time.

864. To walk along a stream.

865. And take in the sun between the trees.

866. A mighty and destructive thing.

867. That makes life possible.

868. From the proper distance and achieves.

869. Such subtleties of feeling on the skin.

870. Of the living.

13. R

871. But we'll live out of order for a long time now.

872. Longer for Maria than for me.

873. If things should happen orderly.

874. It's the most of hope one can muster.

875. As the sun sets on another day.

876. And descends into the earth.

877. Where the dead are buried.

878. To take refuge in the chest of someone for the night.

879. And in the morning rise

880. Without them.

12. I

881. To leave them in an unreachable place.

882. Even as we think hard.

883. About a voice and a face.

884. About an unmistakable gait.

885. Or visit after a few hours of opening gifts.

886. And eating cake.

887. And talking about everything but them.

888. Because it only takes a moment to feel it whole.

889. Another day the mighty can do nothing.

890. For us or to us.

11. A

891. Another day Maria closes her eyes.

892. As she sits on the chair in front of me.

893. Her legs beneath her skirt.

894. And her arms in her lap.

895. As weak as they were on the day she heard the news.

896. That her sister had gone away.

897. Without the strength to move her from one place to the other.

898. Or turn the doorknob to open the door into the room.

899. And see the faces of her father and mother.

900. Like she had never seen them before.

10. M

901. But someone has made plans for the day.

902. And Maria can already see to the end of it.

903. And her legs and arms save any strength they have.

904. For when she returns.

905. From another few hours of being out there.

906. The details of which seem like dust.

907. On the perimeter of an exploding star.

908. To take her up the stairs and into her room.

909. To close the curtains.

910. And pull back the blanket.

9. A

911. To lie there and wait.

912. For the last of the daylight she can see.

913. In the space between the curtain and the window.

914. To go dark.

915. And obscure all nearby debris.

916. A darkness that may end one day.

917. But an end that never will.

918. And me downstairs fiddling with the loose chair leg.

919. Trying to fix it quietly.

920. So she forgets that I'm there.

8. R

921. But I'll remind her in good time.

922. With the gift of a chocolate croissant.

923. Or a bowl of peppers picked from the garden.

924. Left by the sink where sunlight coming through the window.

925. Casts a shadow so that she might not see.

926. The bowl as she turns from the last stair.

927. Her hand letting go of the staircase rail.

928. But moving nearer, past the secretly fixed chair.

929. Past the sofa where I stayed.

930. Recognize the green and orange skins.

7. I

931. And know that it was me.

932. Who went out and picked what was ripe.

933. Before she woke up.

934. Before she sat at her piano and played.

935. The nocturne.

936. Like the sun shines in my dreams.

937. Always dark, always sad.

938. Or what I consider darkness and sadness to be.

939. I'll hear the music from another room.

940. Or outside in the garden.

6. A

941. But over time the piano will go out of tune.

942. And not tuned for her again.

943. Then given to a couple whose daughter.

944. Wanted to take lessons.

945. And set up in their living room.

946. So they could watch her grow and remember.

947. How her feet couldn't reach the pedals.

948. And then one day waking.

949. As if into another dream.

950. Hear a note sustained.

5. M

951. Like an injunction from the future.

952. As the mother cried quietly and the father.

953. Cried without showing it.

954. Each wanting to protect the other.

955. From the thought of death.

956. That comes for them in a moment.

957. And stays too long.

958. When they think of her.

959. Separated from them.

960. As if in another world.

4. A

961. Like a hand that pulls from inside.

962. The heart and bone.

963. Pulling but not pulling through.

964. The veins and arteries to their limit.

965. And only letting go.

966. To pull again another day.

967. Or sometimes the same day.

968. If she'd been gone too long.

969. Or if the house was too quiet.

970. Though she was a quiet child.

3. R

971. And it was difficult to know if she was at home.

972. And then later the visits to see if she was okay.

973. If she remembered her sister's birthday.

974. They had brought a photograph of the two of them together.

975. Not from when they were young.

976. It was too hard to see.

977. Because even in front of them.

978. She restrained herself to the thinnest memory.

979. And only go back a few years.

980. Not all the way.

2. I

981. Those Maria saved for late nights.

982. And early mornings when she played.

983. But after she played.

984. She'd walk to the window and tap on the glass.

985. Just a few because I was already looking.

986. And gesture me to come inside.

987. But before I did, tap again.

988. And point up to the sky.

989. Where a bird circled overhead.

990. The same one from last spring.

1. A

991. And I'd be happy that she saw it first.

992. Because it wouldn't have seemed important if I did.

993. And I wouldn't have pointed in the same way.

994. As if it were something interesting to look at.
995. Or think about instead.
996. Then inside to the kitchen where she and I would sit.
997. Over the photograph of her sister.
998. Taken not so long ago.
999. That she'd left out on the kitchen table.
1000. From the night before.

www.ingramcontent.com/pod-product-compliance
Lightning Source LLC
Chambersburg PA
CBHW031420160426
43196CB00008B/1006